73

Hard Summer

☙

poems by Francisca Matos

Write Bloody UK

www.writebloodyuk.co.uk

First edition.
ISBN: 978-1-8380332-2-4

Cover Design by Luna aït Oumeghar
Interior Layout by Winona León
Edited by Fern Angel Beattie
Author Photo by Gonçalo Fonseca

Type set in Bergamo.

Write Bloody UK
London, UK

Support Independent Presses
writebloodyuk.co.uk

HARD SUMMER

HARD SUMMER

Of course, if we'd been quiet, we would've heard nothing. And that silence, too, would've ruined us.

—Carrie Fountain

HOME TEAM

We still believed in hot lemon water in the morning,
still believed in the miracle of breaking into dance
anywhere, never quieting down, the rookie optimism
that our best parts would remain the same
no matter where or who we shared them with.
Now every summer something like grief stretches inside
our bellies, awakes us with a jolt demanding to know
about betrayal, about abandonment,
so we meet after dinner to look for answers, a search
party in hoodies determined to walk through all of July.
When I think about the summer this is all I see:
my girls and I in the dark curled up into a huddle,
arms stacked, a tight circle for the home team.

NOBODY LAUGHED AT THE CLOWNS

The circus came to the suburbs every year. A large tent set up in the open field. Camels grazed on the dirty grass where years later I would find abandoned needles. This is my first memory, my parents and I squeezed on the wooden bench as the stage lights dimmed for one second before coming on again, announcing its beginning. But I don't remember the show except for the clowns—their ragged faces, make-up melting down flammable clothes. How they tried to win the crowd. I was thinking: I can't fix the silence. I was thinking: if nobody laughs, I'll burst. We didn't stay for much longer. The only other thing I remember is the drive home, my face wet and sore, the tent fading into the distance as we turned away.

It Must Have Been June

from the way the night folded over our bodies,
with the heft of a long Sunday, my mother watching TV,
bare feet on the table, a bowl of forgotten ice cream on her lap.
I was reading in the low amber of our living room,
dog earing questions I would save for much later,
when my grandmother, up again after going to sleep,
marched quietly toward us in her nightgown, wrestled with
her lips and, freeing them with firmness, said: *you don't love me.*
And we didn't do anything, we stood still watching the words
float into the center of the room, the three of us trying
to measure them in our silence. This was before,
before I understood the coldness of the bowl,
the strain of summer, the violent things that keep us awake.

YOU KNOW YOUTH IS INVALUABLE

My friends and I, we're nice kids,
good kids good at being kids,
we show our love by not saying a word.

We stand instead in line waiting for the blow,
and pass on a water bottle in case one of us gets thirsty.

Sometimes it's a Wednesday evening
and there are four bodies slumped on the couch,
other times it's a party,
and more bodies take over the kitchen.

A house party is a party at the house where
we learn to dance or pray or hold a hand,
which really are all the same.

I am in love with exactly twenty people.
Sometimes I wish I could run until the feeling leaves me,
other times I wish I could run towards everyone.

In High School

Death came to us in strange ways, whistled through the corridors, leaked through the metal roofs, curled up like smoke and twisted around the gates, and we were too young to know what it really meant, but didn't want to be left behind in the uncertainty, so when a kid got run over by the train during lunch period, the news travelled fast, and our immediate reaction was to laugh because it seemed impossible and we were still eating, but as soon as the food settled in our stomachs, we were given more details, how he was crossing the tracks on his way back from the beach, how you can't see the train coming from the bend, how his two best friends saw it happening. I say he was run over but in our language it's more like harvested, so after that we were wary of the seasons, of being plucked from the soil, and we watched his friends fight with his girlfriend over a hoodie the next day, over who had the right to wear grief, but we all went to the vigil, marched solemnly to the tracks and stood silent for a minute, and I watched some kids' mouths twitch into an almost grin because, as I said, it still seemed unreal and we didn't know any better, especially not after what happened, months later, when a kid was arrested for murder and the news broke in first period and splattered into very few words, like *his mother* like *his dad found her* like *on the street,* and how he showered and got back to his homework, and my friend told us how she once saw him steal a Starbucks mug on an exchange trip to Scotland, so as you can see, we were pretty tired by summer. But this wasn't everything, there were also the losses that took place outside those gates, and I can't speak for everyone, but in my case it happened on the first day of high school, when I got home and heard my grandfather howl from the living room, so I couldn't tell anyone about my first day and didn't know who to confide in at school the next morning, which kid I could trust with this fragile thing, so when my other grandmother died during Easter break I handled it with the same silence, and summer came like a drowsy wave and I didn't know how to mourn.

SHARING

I want to tell you about my cousin, his story, why it lives in the back of
my mind as if it is my own, maybe because like me, he was never afraid,

maybe like me he was terrified of everything too, but these are
not my memories, I was merely a witness after they happened,

the time he walked away from being robbed at knife-point on his
way home, the secrets I wasn't supposed to know but somehow did,

the pool of blood he left behind at the skatepark on its opening day,
the party over, his jaw wired shut for months. Speaking of blood,

I remember clearly when I realized we shared it. He'd been locked in
the bathroom for over an hour when we went over to visit, no sound

except for a buzz, then the door, then him coming out to the living
room to greet us, his head shaved clean and a bright, gory smile.

SUBURBAN LYRIC

always the rush   the snatching
of the keys   the sprint
out the door   but also time
& its spillage   our clumsy hands
secretly we love it   the waste
something about your friends
my friends   the town
a love letter   leave no one
behind   all of us   upset
lately   it's been summer
for so long

CEREMONY

Some of us are sitting on the couch waiting our turn,
feeling the roughness of our strands, others are dancing,
thinking how different they want to come out of this night,
to leave brand new and changed.

You call out our names from the bathroom like a professional,
trash bag around our necks, shears in one hand and a plastic comb
in the other, from this house that isn't ours, but which has seen our phases.

We stand up straight and ignore the music, smother the laughter,
and let the scissors run close to our ears. We hear the snip
and close our eyes, the reveal is beautiful.

The next morning the house is dormant,
and there are kids passed out in every dusty corner of sunlight.
Our locks are scattered everywhere, blowing golden on the porch.

WHERE WE LIVE

I want to say your house but I think I mean you,
who leaves the front door open and goes back
to your video game, knowing it won't take long
for everyone to arrive and trip on each other's shoes.
I want to say we come here because we're bored
but I think I mean hungry or lonely.
I think I'm here because this is my favourite sound,
a chorus of screams and laughter erupting through
the living room, I mean, what's more suburban
than a fistful of slack-jawed boys crammed together
on the couch? What's more love than not asking questions
and passing the controller instead?
For years you've been sleeping on your couch
rather than your own bed, folding the blankets and
propping up the pillows before anyone needs a seat.
I think I know why. I think I would do the same.

There Isn't Enough Time for a Good Ending

all the girls are quiet
all the girls are in the car looking through the window
all the girls are hoping the next song will match their mood
all the girls are pretending they're in a movie
all the girls are crying in the dark of a concert room
all the girls reach their hands to the front row
all the girls close their eyes when the music dips
all the girls take the long way home in the early morning
all the girls are hungry
all the girls tuck their hair behind their ears
all the girls are serious about the love they're offering
all the girls are planning their escape from their hometowns
all the girls are fighting over who loves the other most
all the girls are waiting by their friend's house

the engine running   feet hovering over the gas pedal
they are wearing their softest clothes

I TELL THIS STORY IN THE CAR

I spot them across the dead grass—
three girls twirling, dizzy on a small wall,
holding each other's wrists.
The girls squeak when they jump,
cheer when they land, pretend
it was the hardest thing they've done
and do it again.

SPRING BREAKERS (2012)

We turn cartwheels in hallways, practice headstands
in pyjama shorts and shoot each other with water guns filled
with things we don't mean. We do our accounting on shop floors,
pennies spilled over cheap crop tops, and refuse to sit apart,
our ponytails nestled together in the back of the bus.

It rains on the first day of our trip and the swimming pool swells.
We browse through the four channels available, stomachs soft on the couch,
legs draped over each other. One day our mouths will surprise us with what
they've kept, and we'll hurl and heave the rocks stuck at the bottom of our bellies,
but for now, we whisper a sigh of relief that, somehow, we made it here.

The sky begins to clear when we settle on a maternity show—
hippo calves sliding out from the womb in a slow-moving river,
zebra foals alive for an hour and already racing, fuzz stuck to their necks.
We agree on not eating animals, in preserving their bodies the same way
we try to preserve ours. We agree on the wrongs of our parents,
but admit the possibility of not doing any better ourselves.

We stare at a montage of kids running in a field, so much green
you can't see where it ends, and one of us asks if we think
we'll stay friends forever. The field must smell so good, like wet grass.

THIS REALLY HAPPENED

It was high noon and the suburbs were scalding.

Everyone had gone home and left their bikes burning silver on the curb.

Except for some lousy birds and the high-voltage buzz of August
there was only the sound of our footsteps.

We were walking around the neighbourhood. We were doing our usual rounds.

As we made a turn towards the stream, two girls cut us off,
unaware of our presence.

They didn't see us and we couldn't move. We stayed frozen.
Our t-shirts stuck to our backs.

I couldn't turn to face her, but felt her shoulders tighten in a way that told me
all I needed to know.

I understood that we had just walked past us. My temples pooled with sweat.

Hours passed. Trust me, they did. The sun was reversing when we finally left.

They looked like they knew where they were headed and we let them go
off into the dusk.

HIGH SEASON

Of all the versions we've shared,
the ones we've kept, and those whispered
to new friends wanting to love us,
this is what I know to be true:
The sun split open for a year.
We ran through days
in the beasts of our bodies.

I need to protect these clementines
from the passage of time

—Chessy Normile

Euro Cup, 2016

Here's what you need to understand: we all needed a win that summer. By we
I mean me, the boys, my girls and our parched country, our sulking land

with its hands under the table, crushed knuckles and tanned, twitching knees,
a nervous laughter capable of lasting through overtime. The hands become

fabric become flags calling for the final whistle, for joy's uncontained shrill.
And when it finally happens, we leave all our things on the floor and exit

with just our beating bodies. And someone's voice asks where we should go,
and the men on the radio clench their microphones, say *anywhere, anywhere but home.*

REPRISE

And when it finally happens—because it has to, because,
like most things, it is not a mistake, not the wrong call made
by the referee's hands but a real win—the city cracks itself open to me.
But I don't stay. I don't hop on the bike and sit by the pier until dawn,
watching morning creep up in layers of blue, then yellow, then orange.
I don't walk down an expensive avenue making guesses at the price
of things, killing time until the first train home, or the next one.
Not yet. I go home with the boys, who spent the last half hour
searching for me, and who, when they finally find me at a crossroads
with a shadow and said bike, the public garden a midnight stage,
will absolutely not leave me behind, a girl in the mouth of adventure.
On our way back to the suburbs, we weave through fireworks and TV
crews and people raising statues for all of us winners. I lay down on
the backseat with my eyes closed, the way a child would just to be
carried into bed. Nothing costs us the game and there is still time.

PRELUDE

How do you tell a story you can barely remember except
for some loose fragments? What do you do with a memory
that is blurry in its truth but folded in the body all the same?
Let me tell you where I was before we won.

★

I follow him into someone's apartment. There are picture frames
littered throughout the living room, souvenirs of a family
I have never met. These are not my boys and they do not
know me, I'm just the one who passes over the ashtray like
I'm eager to serve. There's only so much I can give. My eyes
drift to a photo of a woman I assume is someone's mother.
Suddenly, I am afraid she will come home early from work
and find me there, what she would think of me, and I hold onto
my clothes, ready to leave. Nobody in this room loves me.

★

I work at a film festival for two weeks and there's a party at the end,
but he has other plans for us, with more people I don't know,
and makes me choose. I pick right and I watch him walk away,
the sound of banged up trash cans echoing through the dark.
I don't follow him and he disappears for a week. He does this
until I learn.

★

I follow him to his apartment but he shuts the door behind him.
I do what I've learned to do best and I beg his shoes,
I beg the door, but neither let me in. This is not the first time
this happens—sometimes I am the one locked in,
in a room that might have been golden but is now empty
of any warmth. I try not to panic. If I behave, I'll be let out sooner,
so instead I picture exactly where I left my stuff,
ready to run once I hear him fumbling for the key.
It doesn't matter if I'm left out or kept in, I am always
being grounded for my devotion, for whatever teen girl
still remains pulsing in me.

*

When I bump into my friends, when I speak to my mother again,
when I refuse to follow, he calls me weak and I agree,
but this time not for the same reasons. Summer is around
the corner and I've missed the suburbs, but there's still
so much city left to see, and someone who doesn't know me,
but wants to, asks me if I'm tired. I'm given the choice I want
and I take it.

BONNIE AND CLYDE (1967)

We weren't the real deal, dishevelled
and beautiful, meant to go out together.
We didn't have any accomplices or friends.
There was no ambush, no pack of rangers
out on the land looking for us. In fact,
no one was looking for me, which might explain
why I stayed for all those months.
Understand that, up until then, my life
hadn't been very lucrative in the currency of love.
Imagine me, giddy with this new mobility,
getting in the car and trusting his experience.
Thinking of us as partners, but also of him
as someone who could teach me how to live.
I followed behind in my untrained body,
until I watched his exploits become violent.
I noticed his hands curl, his face change every time
he caught me looking back through the rearview mirror.
So I did what we'd practised in case of danger.
I opened the door of the moving Ford,
the road sharp underneath me, and
jumped onto the gravel. Had I kept going,
I wouldn't have made it very far.

AND WHERE WERE YOU THAT SUMMER

I was wide awake. Tearing oranges apart, pulp and dirt under my fingernails.
Stuffing slices into everyone's mouths hoping to be loved the right way.
My hands always sticky. My skirts always too short to climb onto rooftops,
but the boys pulled me up so I could have a taste of the city, the real one.
That was the summer my girls were gone. The summer I scaled trees like I'd
spent my whole life doing it, dangling my bare legs in the dark until a cop
made us come down, ignoring the boys and looking directly at me, telling me
to go home as if he knew I didn't belong there, never would, kissing in the shadows
trying to outgrow something I could not name. I already knew then you could
only keep up with so much, that come fall I would stop talking to the boys
and by winter avoid the parks we slept in altogether. Years later,
I am peeling oranges for people I might love. I am wide awake. There's a green
fire escape in the back of my mind, an empty bench, a fountain that's since
dried out. And I think I want to be there again, but all I want is the memory,
its roundness heavy in my hands.

THE FILM CREW

The boys and I are shooting a short. It doesn't have a clear plot yet
and in fact, it never will, but we're too familiar with the season's tendency
towards abandonment to care, plus we are a little bored and eager. All I know
is that for the next few days I'll respond to the name Suzie, and play chess
in a decisive match with another girl, who is their close friend and chill,
so really, it's her I'm trying to impress. The heatwave shows no signs
of stopping any time soon. This is the fourth time we are shooting
the opening scene, Suzie arriving at a bar at noon on a vintage bike,
approachable, but not too smiley. Suzie isn't afraid of the camera
or looking messy, which is why everything she does looks good,
which is why I keep getting off the bike and rolling it up the street to
my mark until I nail it. I do this so many times I get hot and flustered.
I want to be her so badly, to let go of my bad habit of caring too much
that I keep going, even after we lose the light and the boys stop recording.
Eventually it works. I know this because later, after dinner and drinks,
I take over one of the couches and let myself fall asleep,
the entire film crew watching.

ROAD MOVIE

Look over there,
that is where the city ends.
I can tell we're not
going anywhere.

We Left Mostly Unscathed

came out of the sun with blood in the neck, crawled into the shadow, tasted the asphalt. The city was coming down—that's how we knew it was fall, that's how we knew defeat. The walk home was different, I had nothing to say about it. When I arrived, my girls were back, bags by their feet, faces knotted in silence. We sat on my steps, arms wrapped around our ankles. The day was growing. I could feel an orange in my pocket. I touched it briefly but didn't dare to look.

SMOOTH TALK (1985)

Connie, I feel like you're one of us. One of my girls alive
and furious, hot blooded and ready for love. We too used to run
breathless across the highway and shriek with every car that came too close.
Who knows why we did it, it was never about the goal but the urge
to make something, anything happen. I admire your elaborate schemes to spend
the days tanning by the sea. I also like what you did with your clothes,
how they looked one way at home and another away from it. I want to say
we learned from you, but I think we are born with this kind of knowledge.

Connie, did you forgive your mother? Like mine,
she must've forgiven you, for all the times you came back distracted
and empty-handed. The times you thought of the farmhouse as inescapable
and longed to be far away from it, somewhere you had never been.
When you stayed behind and missed the family barbecue, I could tell
you were lonely by the way you sat on the staircase and lowered the radio.
I've missed out on so many things. Like me, you're a victim of time.

Connie, there was a man too. First, it was intriguing but then
I felt that familiar sense of danger flutter in the belly. Quickly,
the farce became apparent, thin and clear as a screen door. You think
you're smart and then you find yourself stranded at a mall parking
garage, rushing to the street towards the nearest payphone, or in my case,
alone in an empty city, trying to get home before sunrise. Us girls,
we always walk in the end. We always barely make it out of the night
with our hearts intact.

Connie, I lied. This habit I picked up from you.
It wasn't a highway for us, not a farmhouse either, and looking back,
the man was really a boy when held closely against the light. But everything
was real. All of it happened and I turned out fine, but there are things
I don't know how to speak of. I wasn't the same when I returned.
I know you know all of this. I knew you would understand.

THE STAKEOUT

In a dream it's that time of day between dinner and death,
when the streetlamps grow amber and the dogs impatient.
I'm bored, wandering around my bedroom like a museum,
weighing the objects in my hands as if I work here and
it's my job to make sure the artefacts are spotless and safe.
I'm organising some photos. I'm cleaning the rocks I brought
from the beach. I'm sorting through old movie tickets,
when B. storms in, mismatched pyjamas under her hoodie,
hair still damp, and she says *I found them. I didn't see them,*
but I heard someone did, they must be close. What are you doing,
where are your shoes? It takes me a second to realise that
she is referring to us, but once I do, I slide my feet into a pair of
flip flops, blurt something to my parents and we head into the night.
The streets are suspiciously empty and we shiver every time
a tree rustles in the wind. We light the path in front of us with
our phones and look for clues, evidence that we are out here
and not somewhere faraway, but all we find is some dirty confetti
sprinkled on the road. B. looks tired. My feet are burning but
we keep walking. We rummage through someone's bushes.
We dig through someone's trash. We dust off our hands
and catch our reflection in a window, beneath the orange light,
the shade of the frame splintering our faces. B. grabs my hand.
Can't stop, she says, *we have to go.*

EASY RIDER (1969)

—A man went looking for America. And couldn't find it anywhere.

when did you notice   was it early in the journey
what gave it away   was it the planes   splitting
the tarmac in half   because I hear them   all the time
they sound the same way   the air tastes sometimes
thick with promise   like something is coming
when you cast off your watch   jumped on your bike
the metal glinting in the desert   I didn't laugh
I took it seriously   sometimes   I am committed
to the metaphor too   your friend is running loose
my friends are dreaming   I'm trying to enjoy myself
what else can I do   but trust the seasons   naturally
this is easier said than done   you know this better than me
you kept going   you made it just in time for the party
so I kept going   trampled over july like I wanted to win it
and in the end   there was nothing   what I'm trying to say is
we all went looking   some of us   are still looking

We watched until our eyes glowed with the dark, kept watch for what we could no longer see clearly in the distance.

—Kim Kent

ON THE CUSP OF SUMMER

Have you noticed all we do is sit around and wait?
We are always sitting, we are always waiting for the slow fade
of the day, for the warm dusk. Do you also imagine
a final scene, an end to this wait? Does it look like running,
your legs tired but strong, mouth full of spit, skin red and blotchy?
Or maybe you are pedalling your bike down the street at sundown,
your back illuminated, your hands tender from pushing down
on the handles, lungs at full capacity.
I think it might end with a dance, with our limbs shapeshifting
into animals in the dark of a friend's living room.
In my first year of college, I worked as a secretary at a film festival.
I spent three days helping a professor from Florida use our computers.
I watched a lot of movies. I got to go to the parties.
On the final day everyone was spread out on the velvet sofas,
hungover from the night before. The professor was holding a paper cup
and I asked if he'd had a good night. He said *I saw you.*
You were dancing but you weren't smiling. It was funny
because it was true. Anyway, has anyone ever seen you?
I was the happiest I've ever been in class on the cusp of summer,
the room dark and overheated and everyone resting on their folded arms,
lulled by Swedish murmurs and the rickety projector.
My saddest memory is walking home after that party.
It was early morning, and everyone was sleeping.
I turned the keys slowly and tiptoed inside.
My room was bathed in pale blue and I sat very still on my bed.
I fell asleep and dreamt of Florida. Hey—
Do you ever worry that pretty soon there'll be
nowhere left to go here? Do you ever just worry?
I am constantly waiting. I care so much,
but I love this song, let's go back inside.

Prank Call

Now when I come back something in my sternum unfastens
the way a bike chain can slacken abruptly mid-ride. A bike chain
can fall off completely, but oftentimes it only becomes loose
and I am propelled towards chaos, I want to keep going until
all the metal comes apart, leaving behind me a trail of wind chimes
sure to awaken everyone. In the morning, they will find all
my missing parts gleaming on the road. If it isn't too loose,
you can keep cycling until your destination and then tighten it,
the chain, but I am not ready to leave until I see everyone I have
ever known. I keep thinking of what I would say to them.
I keep thinking that if I prank called everyone I have ever loved,
they would pick up the phone and recognise my breathing,
my well-intentioned giggle before I inevitably hang up.
I am convinced I could pull this off: write a coded message,
hide some coordinates in between the lines. They would lead
to an empty field or a parking lot after hours. I would arrive early
and wait patiently for a dozen tall kids to show up. Then,
I could finally speak. I would say *thanks for coming, goodnight.*

THE ONLY TIME I LET MYSELF FEEL IT

was on a national holiday in a square full of people
singing about freedom with carnations stuck to their chests,
so it wasn't weird to be crying really, but the truth is
I was crying because someone was dead, gone the night before,
and because it was a teacher, the kind who waits for everyone
to leave at the end of class to trust you with a good movie,
and because we never really talked except in email,
and because I couldn't hold grief, I obsessed over her inbox,
swam through the marching crowd until I recognised someone
from the summer, grabbed their shoulders and blurted
if they knew what happened to dead people's email accounts,
and they said *I don't know* and I asked *who knows?*
and they handed me their half-empty beer cup,
and I clenched it with my teeth because by that point
my hands were gone, and later in the evening,
after I dragged myself home, after I missed the wake,
I thought about everyone who was gone and fell asleep in
front of the TV with *PARIS, TEXAS* on, Harry Dean Stanton saying
a vacant lot...I thought we might live there someday.

WATCHING *GIRLS* WITHOUT YOU

I understand why it is so,
why time has to be trimmed to fit
the medium, measured in episodes,
I know next week the writers will give us
another bite and we'll see the girls bumping
into each other at an art show, in line for
frozen yoghurt at lunchtime, or at someone's
engagement party. I know they will be hurt
but equally relieved at the sight of each other,
they will gesture at the bride, the groom they've
never met as if to say *this is crazy, I can't believe this is happening,*
and they will both laugh, shrug it off and dance
until the early hours. Then, they will walk home barefoot
clutching their shoes, and the credits will roll
with the perfect song to show that this
is the real love story. Don't get me wrong,
I love it. This is the only kind of love in which
I'm certain I truly believe. But mostly, I am interested
in the in-between bits, the parts that aren't ever
scripted, just implied, before they meet again.
I don't buy the nonchalance—that the girls
would go on with their lives as if nothing happened,
without so much as finding themselves lonely in
the afternoon, clutching their chests, trying to
extract the peach pit stuck inside. I don't believe
they would enjoy their meals or listen to music
or dress nicely. Every conversation would be
frivolous and fleeting. I guess what I am trying
to say is that I don't like the gap, not knowing
what will happen. I don't know how to be cool,
which is why I am at your door demanding answers,
asking you to text me back.

FROM MEMORY

After they first cured her and before they couldn't,
my grandmother climbed the edge of a too-soft armchair,
reached her arms to the top of the bookshelf
and came back down with her notebook in hand, ready.
My grandfather, sensing her voice shake from the other room,
knowing too well what was about to unfurl in her mouth,
stormed in furious and yanked the poems from her hands.
Lately I've been trying to remember what happened next,
how it ended, but all I have is a half-formed story.
Maybe she snatched them back and started
reading, voice rising through the room.
Maybe she recited from memory, right hand raised
as if conducting, looking at me straight.
Maybe she was teaching me.

GREY GARDENS (1975)

In another life, we would share a stage.
You would parade around in your best outfit,

black stockings, tight leotard, scarf around your head
(your hair grown back into curls in the new air)

and I would sing about us, the epic of our impossible feat,
how we left our old bedrooms and never looked back.

In between acts, you would beckon the audience to
look at us, to really take a good look at our faces,

wise and radiant, seasoned in the act of letting go,
and the night would roll and end in roaring applause,

with a standing ovation and red fleshy roses at our feet.
Of course, we would have different names, no longer

turn our heads to our mothers' call. We couldn't
tell our friends. The only way this life could work

would be if we uncoiled from our memories completely,
and moved to a city with too many people to recognise anyone.

It's difficult to dream, isn't it? So difficult already
to live between what was and what is.

Some things are inescapable, so I guess I should still
call you Little Edie. When you said that in your youth

you had to give up the three things you cared about,
the Catholic church, dancing and swimming, I understood.

Still when I read how you spent your last days, swimming
alone in the Floridian sea, I was relieved you hadn't quit.

And I wondered if you were breast stroking towards something
bright, or just doing some laps before coming back to shore.

Director's Cut

I don't know how to live in a way that makes sense,
how to love everything I love without checking if we got
everything right—the colours, the faces, the voices.
If the light is good. If the music is really good.

I'm always half-way in remembering, foot through the door of memory,
trying not to run around the set so no one can accuse me of being messy.

No one ever does. Everyone is dancing and I'm always invited.
I don't know what to tell you, I loved everything so much I smudged
the negatives like a careless child and left them out in the sun,
I never wanted the party to end so I left early.

Sometimes I'm folded in the moment, not stuck inside memory's
coating, but then I wake up worried about the morning reviews,
forget that no one ever reads them. Maybe I'm afraid of forgetting.
Maybe this was about my hands all along, how I have to drop the camera,
how I can't hold anymore.

Running Lessons

Lately we've been going on runs,
leaving the flat in our ponytails and
chanting like a real track team to the river.
Nicole rolls her shoulders and declares
we're on a path to healing, then crouches
down midway. I break off on my own,
race myself like I've had it in me all this time,
something, and who knows if that's true,
but I hear Julia yell in her coach voice
that Nicole should dig deep so I dig too,
and later, when we regroup to head home,
make a turn past the college and zig zag
through the tourists, a security guard will
look at us panting and laugh—
I can feel my heart ripping apart, I blurt with spit in my throat
You're doing so good, she says.

How Long Until Summer Now?

This morning I let the sun deceive me.
I didn't adjust to its brightness but rather let it flood my desk,
where I lay my head long enough for my scalp to catch on fire.
My body is heavy with remembering. On days like this
I lug it to the balcony floor and sit very still, watching planes
slice the sky gently as if not to disturb the memory.
In the memory, it's absurdly warm and I have things to do,
but I dig my elbows into a patch of grass and stay suspended
in the hum of the city. Only tourists would dare to walk.
On days like this I don't dress for the weather. I leave my flat
in my thinnest clothes and pretend it's not still January.
The truth is I miss everyone. But I think this makes me
the lucky one, to feel the cold on my ankles, the faint heat
pulling me by the sleeves.

In the Future, I Love the Future
after Olivia Gatwood

Every morning, a morning. A cup of lemon water.
I'm still the first one to rise but now I am also the first

to fall asleep. The sunlight fractures my face but it doesn't
hurt. The weather is what it wants to be and I don't sulk,

I don't pace nervously in front of the window thinking of
who it reminds me of that day. I still remember everything.

I still wear the same clothes but empty my pockets of memories,
no longer wait to see how far they can skid before they sink.

No more water up to my knees. First, I was sad knowing
things would end and then I was inconsolable when they did,

but now I am ready for nothing. I have future in excess.
I don't know how I got here, but the music is good and unfamiliar.

I can't tell the tempo but I'm an excellent dancer, all muscle
and pulse. I can be the last one standing. I have no plans.

There's laughter coming from the kitchen or the balcony.
I don't hear my name, but I follow the sound.

THE PICTURES HOLD

The feeling never goes away. It stays carefully tied around these scenes.
They come to me in dreams where I'm walking and stopping,
and then running, and running, and running

Deleted Scenes

I.

days we floated in blue chlorine / our bodies soft / our heads heavy / our bright eyes / set on the sun / swimming to the tiled bottom / and holding the weight down / with both arms / when we come out / we adjust the fabric / walk back to our towels / and bury our faces / until our skin is dry / and red / I leave the apartment complex / damp tote bag chafing my hip / the birds and my flip flops / there is something about girls / screaming underwater / something about them / always coming back up / to breathe

II.

days when the sky was a grey window / the sea too wet / for the body to touch / the air a still balm / we sat down on damp denim / plucking nothings out of the earth / tall grass poking under our shorts / beyond the hedges / a lonely car passes by / a dog barks in the distance / all the kids are either bored / or dying / at some point / we learn something / about days like these / drugged / and wasted / the evening a looming thing / we don't feel good here

III.

days when the sun was a swollen welt / the street an impossible setting / silver playground / we decide to walk anyway / eyes down / shoulders exposed / sweat dripping from our temples / the backs of our necks defeated / the truth hurts less / when you're dizzy / even if you're certain / the cars are truly burning / in the distance / not an illusion / just the way things bubble / in the heat / but we are still soft here / and so loud / we talk over the crackle / leave the hard bits for later / alone / in our pastel bedrooms / peeling off the dead skin

IV.

days when the movies / were the perfect hideout / from the heatwave / air-conditioned bliss / we sat in the dark for hours / goose-bumped arms / knees pulled in / we love horror the best / the kind with an old house / unruly yard / and girls who dare to break in / sundresses wrinkled / flashlights in hand /we love hauntings / spirits who mess with the lights / turn on the radio at 3 a.m. / the music growing tenser / and louder / we squeeze each other's knuckles / giggle through the jump scares / we aren't afraid of the house / of some jealous ghost / we are scared for the girls / what happens to them after / when they leave at the end

V.

days we sat together / on the living room carpet / barefoot and thirsty / elbows resting / on the shaggy cushions / we don't want to go outside / too much light / too much of the same thing / we are sick of the beach / and of everyone / who isn't sick of it yet / can't they see it's not a mirror / can't they see it's a faulty clock / diary entries we write / for other people to read / we wear serious faces / flicking through the music channels / until we find something / we recognize / we sing the chorus / mimic the choreography / of course we are sick of it / but of course / we don't say it

VII.

days we didn't know / didn't think / it would get so cold / the kind of wind / that made you weak / to the bone / no matter how tough / you tried to be / this place looks sincere / in the dark / this place sounds peaceful / just our footsteps / and the clink from inside our bags / we make it to the park / and sit in a circle / we don't notice / the houses around us / flicking their lights / to send us home / we didn't know / didn't think / it would get this cold / is it that we came unprepared / or that we're still pretending / to believe / in our mouths

VIII.

days when it didn't matter / what we said / our voices muffled / by the heavy rain / pouring in loud thumps / flooding the school / lifting us / off the ground / floating girls / can't remember / how we got here / never learned / the language of truth / we don't look each other in the eye / we look down at our feet / our dirty shoes / the canvas is fading / the rubber is cracking / the laces are tied / in a difficult knot

IX.

days we couldn't remember / what the sun felt like / hands buried inside our coats / noses pink and wet / we're all dressed up on the train / bottles between our feet / like ritual / like we can't have fun / without spilling things first / when we get to the pier / it's almost midnight / and the crowd is waiting / time / swallows us whole / the sky finally / cries out fireworks

X.

days we did everything / to be left behind / on the way home / a different turn / a longer walk / slow paced / past the shallow stream / just to end up / where we started / the high school gates / are pale blue / we are old / but full of want / like dogs / always loyal / always alert / sometimes we cry / with our mouths open / stray and starving / all demanding / to be loved / say / i don't think / we'll ever leave / ever not whimper / when the sun goes down

ACKNOWLEDGEMENTS

Thank you to the editors of the following journals, which first published these poems:

"Home Team"— *Vagabond City*

"Spring Breakers (2012)" (formerly titled "Spring Breakers Forever") — *Feels Zine*

"Euro Cup, 2016" and "Reprise" — *Electric Literature*

I am so grateful to Fern Angel Beattie and Write Bloody UK for taking a chance on me and my work.

Thank you to my tutors Maura Dooley and Stephen Knight for your invaluable guidance. I am forever indebted to my teacher Margarida Vale de Gato — thank you for seeing me before I did.

Thank you to my family for constantly encouraging me to pursue what I want.

This is a book about memory. It is also a book about friends.

Thank you to Oliver Sedano-Jones, Rami Farawi, Rhys O'Connor and João Gabriel Palaio for your patience and support, for reading the many versions of these poems and helping me make this book what it is now. Above all, thank you for your friendship.

Thank you to Lillis Hendrickson for looking after me. To Nicole Fersko for your love. Thank you to Julia DeBenedictis for your endless encouragement and loud enthusiasm, and for always knowing exactly what I mean.

Thank you to Beatriz Martins and Rita Fernandes for choosing me as your friend that day and growing up with me — the real home team. To Marta Nogueira, Bernardo Maciel and Laís Gilioli for raising me.

Thank you to Paloma Moniz for, more than anything, our wild and dramatic love story. To Ricardo Gonçalves for always showing up. I owe a lot to the two of you — thank you for leaving your door open to me.

To Gonçalo Fonseca for taking the train back to the suburbs with me that night and always being around since.

Thank you to Bruno for dreaming this and everything else with me. For always telling me to go.

Finally, to all the K-spot kids — this book is for you. Thank you to Miguel Alves for keeping us together.

Write Bloody would like to give special thanks to angel donor Sohrab Mehta

About the Author

FRANCISCA MATOS is a poet from Lisbon, Portugal. Her work has been featured in *Feels Zine*, *Vagabond City*, *Wax Nine Journal* and *Electric Literature*, among others. She holds an MA in Creative & Life Writing from Goldsmiths, University of London and is the recipient of a Fulbright scholarship, as well as the Jane Cooper fellowship from Sarah Lawrence College, where she will pursue her poetry MFA.

IF YOU LIKE FRANCISCA MATOS, FRANCISCA LIKES...

What We Are Given
Ollie O' Neill

Cut To Bloom
Arhm Choi Wild

Floating, Brilliant, Gone
Franny Choi

This Way To The Sugar
Hieu Minh Nguyen

No Matter the Wreckage
Sarah Kay

Bloody beautiful poetry books.

Write Bloody UK is an independent poetry publisher passionate
about bringing the voices of UK poets to the masses.
Trailing after Write Bloody Publishing (US) and
Write Bloody North (Canada), we are committed to
handling the creation, distribution and marketing of our authors;
binding their words in beautiful, velvety-to-the-touch books
and touring loudly with them through UK cities.

Support independent authors, artists, and presses.

Want to know more about Write Bloody UK books, authors, and events?
Join our mailing list at
www.writebloodyuk.co.uk

9 781838 033224